TALES FROM TILL...

CHATS AT THE
SUPERMARKET CHECKOUT

BY

BILL CAWLEY

FIRST EDITION

T M B
BOOKS

First published in Great Britain in 2014
by TMB Books, the publishing arm of the Tripe Marketing Board,
a division of LEB Ltd
57 Orrell Lane,
Liverpool, L9 8BX

ISBN 978-0-9573141-3-9

British Library Cataloguing in Publication Data.
A catalogue record for this book is available from the British Library.

Edited and Designed by Paul Etherington.

Cover illustration by Victuallers, interior illustrations by Charles P, Benno
Bartocha, Lothar Schaack and Roger Rossing (all Wikimedia Commons).

Dedicated to the memory of Sharon Chandler

ACKNOWLEDGEMENTS

I would like to thank my family particularly Cathy who has been so encouraging, Paul Etherington for having confidence in this project, Nick Broadhead and Rose Baxter for proofreading the early drafts of *Tales from the Till* and my fellow USDAW reps who work hard to support our members in the industry.

Finally, I am indebted to all those supermarket workers and customers who might recognise some of the incidents described in this little book, which is offered in the hope that it brightens their day.

PREFACE

 Some time ago, a customer responded to a quote from *Macbeth* I gave by saying "I did not expect an intelligent remark from a supermarket worker". It was a Saturday evening and I mentioned the remark to one of the young women who was working that night. She was incensed. She was working part time to supplement her student finances as she was doing a Chemistry degree at a local university. I suppose this incident illustrates the principal reason why I started to collect some of my encounters with customers.

Supermarket workers are not anonymous people and I, in common with my colleagues, do like some interaction with the customers we endeavour to serve well. *Tales from the Till* was therefore born out of the need to show that retail workers are as interesting people as any that you are likely to meet in a day to day encounter.

Oh and, by the way, most shop workers I have spoken to do not like customers using mobile phones.

I should also add that most experiences with the customers go perfectly well and many of the checkout operators have forged an easy familiarity with shoppers who regularly frequent the supermarket. That was one reason for starting to collect these fleeting conversations.

Another was that, although the majority are light-hearted exchanges, there are some that are poignant and cover a variety of human emotions such as the man who told me that he had just received the "all clear" from cancer, or the woman fearing for her husband in Afghanistan.

In short, it's a one man attempt at a Mass Observation Survey over a period that has included one of the worst recessions in the last 80 years. Its genesis was a series of Tweets or Facebook posts issued after my shifts at the checkout.

I shall end this preface by explaining a little about the town of Leek. It is a pretty market town on the edge of the Peak National Park. A place of few pretensions, it has seen a transformation over the last 40 years as many of the textile mills on which the town depended have closed. Most of the workforce of the town is reliant on low paid work and for many, my colleagues included, life has been difficult in recent years. It is clear to me though that, whatever the uncertainties, my fellow workers have unvaryingly responded to such times with humour and good cheer.

Bill Cawley

CONTENTS

AISLE ONE

Suggested to a 30-something woman that the *Telegraph* was an age restricted product and that she had to be 60 before she could buy it. She got the joke, fortunately.

Couple arrive at my till with DVDs and a choice to be made. She likes rom coms and he likes slasher movies. I suggest compromise film, *Headless in Seattle*.

9

Woman tells me that she was a pirate in a previous life. If she was a pirate she would have bought rum and not Pimms.

The bill came to 16.88. "A good year," man says.
I say "Year of the Glorious Revolution, for some".
"We need a revolution now," he says, "Bring back Oliver Cromwell".
I point out that he banned Christmas.
"True, but no mosques".
He moved on, but I should have said that Old Nolly was liberal on the question of Jews. I think that would have left him puzzled.

Man tells me he pressed wrong button when paying with card. I tell him that it's a good job he's not in charge of British nuclear deterrent.

Man buys cider only and lots of it. He does not appear very healthy. I often get alcoholics who come into the store very early. Their pallor is usually awful.

At work yesterday spoke to woman from Montreal. Other woman further down the line misheard "Did she say that she was a comedian?" "No," I responded "a Canadian".

Man getting excited by my mentioning the Troggs' *Wild Thing* and he does a little dance in front of me. His wife tells me "That will be it now for the rest of the day".

I notice that the disposable nappies were on special offer at £6.66. I wonder if there are any children in the store named Damien.

Elderly woman buys six very large water melons which I put in her trolley for her as she wheels away. It seems an excessive amount. But recall the plot of the 1973 film *Day of the Jackal* about an attempt on De Gaulle when assassin buys water melon to test explosive power of special bullets. Water melon explodes. Perhaps she is planning to bump off Hollander. Should I contact French Embassy?

Woman asked me whether *Thor*
was a good film.
I said that the critics had given it a good
hammering.

Adrian Street the wrestler, I was told by some bloke who saw a documentary on BBC4, "looked like a combination of Emma Bunton and a Welsh coal miner".

Man gruffly says that he can do his own packing. I tell him that it's admirable that the spirit of resourcefulness and derring-do that made the Empire is still there.

Man from Hebburn tells me that sister married a Mackem. Dad took it badly. "Could have been worse," I say "could have been Tory as well".

Beer called *Wyre Piddle* sounds like a urinary tract infection.

Youth asks me at till if we had any *Star Wars* stickers. I tell him "No *Star Wars* stickers, sorry we have".

Woman says that I am going too fast. I pause and ask whether she wants me to go at 33 rather than 45 rpm. I can really slow down to 18 if she wants me to.

"Only decent man to get into Parliament," says man about Guy Fawkes and claims to be an anarchist. He still buys a lot so perhaps the anti-consumerism element may have passed him by. I tried him with a bit of Proudhon just to see whether his anarchism met the test. It didn't.

Wonder when did the fashion that women have for piling up hair that from a distance looks like Mickey Mouse ears start?

I think that the man's accent is Scouse but he is a Mancunian. Wars have been started for less.

Woman wearing Lawn Tennis Association top. I have tried the game once or twice, as I have with hockey when a friend doing her teaching practice taught it to people who have never played the game. I was a natural at it, as I was with croquet - which again, I have only played once. I've got good hand to eye coordination - all the family have it.

Man at work - a customer - I ask how he is and he says ecstatically happy as today he has had the all clear for his bladder cancer. I shake his hand and he is virtually skipping out of the store.

"Your mushrooms have fallen from the belt". It could be a euphemism, I suppose or the opening line of a Captain Beefheart song.

Spoke to woman from Colorado. She was visiting family. She was from the same town as *Mork and Mindy* was filmed. She was proud of this association.

I meet an elderly gent who was buying heather. He'd probably be fined if he took it from the Moors. It seems to be the case if he nicked Sphagnum Moss.

Listening to a quartet in the store café worried about "them" and discussing the fact that the town is the third "whitest" place in the UK. I don't know whether this is a fact. One woman opines the coldness of the north might keep "them" away. The group give off a collective shudder at the prospect of "them" at the gates.

Spoke to work colleague who says that if anyone had told him a decade ago that he needed two jobs to survive he would have laughed. I know others who have three or four.

Man who looks like he is one of the Gumbys. He stands vacant-looking at end of till. His badge proclaims that he works for a local college.

Man from Cromer. I told him that I met this very old chap who was Deputy Town Clerk aged 16 in 1917. He saw 80 ships, of all sorts, in the harbour one day during First World War. We spoke about Henry Blogg who has a statue in Cromer. He was a Cox of the lifeboat who saved over 200 lives and won the George Medal twice. A great Englishman who deserves to be better known and we both agreed on that.

Woman buys *Cockneys v Zombies.* I thought that the words are interchangeable. Read somewhere that teens in East Ham had only 600 words in use. If true there are intelligent chimps that could probably match them.

The bill comes to £18.40. Couple knowing about my reputation ask what happened in 1840? The disgraceful Opium war when we went to war with China over drugs they did not want and on a lighter note it was the year of Victoria's wedding.

Woman buys Yorkshire Rhubarb from Wakefield and Lancashire Tripe. A meal that combines both would test the skills of Ainsley I would think.

Man wears 'Red Wedge' tee shirt rather influenced by Kandinsky. Told him to look it up.

Goat's milk: a man buys a lot and it would be easier for him to buy a goat, which I suggest. And, I add, if Satan wanted a devilish creature he could have selected something less ridiculous than a goat.

Spoke to bloke who talks to me about bands. I saw Frank Zappa's albums in a local Oxfam including *Weasels Ripped My Flesh*. Hoxton came into the conversation as well for some reason and I mentioned the Krays.

Daily Express has an article about decent Britons. I am firmly in the camp of the indecent Britons if I am measured by what the *Daily Express* means by decent.

I had that Leo Tolstoy at my till last night. He bought rye bread, salt and vodka. The big white beard was a giveaway. To quote Groucho Marx "Don't point that thing at me it might go off". Still, I suppose, I ought to be honoured that the back-from-the-dead Russian writer should want to use my till. Come to think of it some years back I had Samuel Beckett at the till although he was not a great talker. Great writers both, but not as good as Nastikoff.

I am on the end till and it is night. The light reflects off my head and I conclude that they have me as a beacon to attract trade or warn passing ships.

Discussed tripe with a woman from Rochdale - it seems her mother used to dress it. Gracie Fields was born just around the corner from her house.

Three Polish families come through the tills one after another. Man with little English loses wallet and goes home. Returns - still no wallet. He is panicking and unloads his rucksack frantically. Turns it upside down and shakes. Wallet falls out. There is a huge look of relief on his face. I suggest that he has a swig of the cherry vodka that he has.

Man buys a meat pie, four cans of lager
and a girly magazine.
It looks like an afternoon in then.

Magazine informs me that Chantelle is
looking for a lippo, or is that a hippo?
Who is Chantelle anyway?

We were having a chat about characters. One of the regulars, a Londoner from Acton, was having a chat about London in the 70s when he lived in the capital and worked for London Transport. I know London well and we spoke of our favourite bits as well as characters. I liked Camden and used to visit the place a lot. He lived for a time in Spitalfields and mentioned Boudicca Redd - a local character in the East End. The next man was also a lover of London and said he used to drive a lorry down the A1 before the motorway was built. He said he had seen some sights in the 60s. I was intrigued.

Woman has writing on her left thigh. It's from
Romeo and Juliet she tells me. The passage reads
'the world will be in love with night'.
How romantic, I think.

A rather short-tempered Eastern European who was tutting and ramming her trolley into the legs of the elderly couple who were moving slowly out of her way. I would have thought she would be used to the principle of queuing given her age and nationality.

Woman had same basket since she was 14 although straps, bottom and side are replacements. Think we are moving into Trigger and broom territory here.

Belfast woman, good natured although originally I think she is a Scot. She has money back. I warned her against being profligate and being a good Ulster Protestant. She acknowledged my concern.

Woman who works for a local vets. I ask her what is the most unusual pet she has worked on and she says a chameleon. They apparently go black when they get annoyed.

News came through that unemployment is up again. The front page of the local newspaper headlines with local food bank opening. A woman tells me that she worked as a volunteer on one in Hull and many of the people receiving the parcels were middle aged, single men who had no family and were on benefits/long term unemployed. I know from experience how hard it is to get any sort of a job. To reduce many previously hard working people to a state of penury is an appalling thing to do.

Man does not have money although a friend lends him some. I feel like wishing the release of the hounds in the manner of Montgomery Burns. I tell him that we give customers ten yards start.

Talked to a woman who has just opened a shop in the town and she was full of high hopes and I wished her good luck.

Man with 'International Brigade' tee shirt came in. His company are doing pro-Republican tee shirts. I recall the slogan from Nationalist General Astray '¡Abajo la inteligencia, Vive la Muerte', (Down with intelligence, long live death). It might be the motto of a certain local authority not too far away. I tell him of someone I knew who went to a Christian Brothers' school near Melrose who nicked the war memorial in the school chapel dedicated to the memory of the boys who died fighting for the Generalissimo. The school also had a head of pastoral care called Brother Discipline.

Woman tells me with obvious pride that her daughter has just won a place at a music college to study the flute. I wondered if she performs standing on one leg in the manner of the bloke out of Jethro Tull. Just a thought and one I would not share with her.

Bait *Daily Mail* reader with Swiftian suggestion that the children of the unemployed might be turned into cat food. I have also been known to say "Assalam ʿalaykum" to readers of the *Mail* or the *Express*. They usually nod and go on their way oblivious to what I have said.

Man loses wallet down tight body warmer. He convulses and wiggles like H Houdini trying to get out of a straightjacket. It takes some time but eventually the wallet drops to the floor.

Holidaymakers at my till who are from The Fens. "Those strange things surrounding the town are hills," I tell them.

Man wearing tee shirt which has what I think is 'Berlin' on it. It isn't. It spells 'BER' and then the lettering changes. "You can call me berk if you want". "If you like," I reply.

Customer in store suggests section for witches. "Sorry we've sold out of liver of blaspheming Jew, but there's a special on hands of glory". Sometime later I saw someone wearing a Pentagram. Perhaps it's getting around the Wicca Community.

Swiping cards noted that bloke was called Nielson. He is Swedish.
"Are you from Malmo?" I guess.
"Yes. Do I have a Malmo face?" he asks.
Better than a Gothenburg chin I reply.

I am on the 'basket only' till and it was unusually quiet. The people with very full trolleys cast spaniel eyes at me when I have no custom although people want a till for a quick shop with just a wire basket. I occasionally let a pensioner through with a trolley if there are only a few items in it. I realise that displaying initiative in this manner is very un-British and I will probably get rebuked.

Spoke to woman ecstatically happy that her bloke was back from Afghanistan. He got back in the early hours and she stayed up and was consequently tired but happy. It's his last tour and he was in the Lancashire Regiment. A colleague had been killed. Her chap does not talk about the conflict. She did say that she thought that the war was a waste and had no confidence in the Afghan authorities. She was of the opinion that the Taliban would be in control within months of the Allies leaving.

A man asks me to pack his bags as he lost a finger in an accident at work many years ago. The company that made wire were negligent. The union helped him to get sizable compensation. If it was not for Trades Unions where would we be? A point I try to bang home to my fellow workers.

AISLE TWO

A discussion on how strange Biddulph Moor is.
Man buys bundles of sticks for heater or is it to
engage in witch burning?

I have sold a new brand of cheese called
Colliers. Pity that there are no pits left for
the Colliers to eat the cheese in.

One-eyed, leering Rumanian appears with girlfriend and begins to fondle her breasts in front of me. I know he is Rumanian as I ask to see ID and he shows me his passport. Of course it could be his sister and Borat might be correct after all.

Man moved from Droylsden to Leek. Could not be happier. No more car alarms, no more helicopters overhead, no more shouts in the night of "Hit him, Tracey".

A discussion on necromancy and the skills of Dr John Dee was followed a little later by an exchange with a couple of Pentecostal preachers. Pressed a tract on me which advises that I can be washed in the blood of the Lamb. Ever likely, the poor thing is looking a little peaky.

Family on holiday renting a house in the moors, they like it. They are from Redcar. The last resort, as someone from the place called it.

Reg, the former security bloke, has a list of records that he hates hearing over the supermarket system. They include *Lyin' Eyes* by The Eagles, anything by Billy Joel, *Christmas Time* by Cliff Richard, and that really annoying *Hello* one with the young Canadian woman with the whimpering voice. I agree with him on that one.

Man just returned from New York a place that I love. I liked the Greenwich Village and Soho areas when I went in the late 90s. He was not impressed with the city although did like going around Ground Zero, an answer that I found depressing.

Over 100 files linked to child sex allegations naming senior establishment figures missing since 80s. Wonder how many files linked to Miners' strike are unaccounted for? I tell sympathetic customer who takes the opportunity to rail at the establishment.

Tell man who buys Vitamin C tablets about origin of 'limey'. He certainly won't be developing scurvy. It leads to a discussion on the 18th century Navy and operations on pitching, poorly-lit vessels in the dark. Surgeon took seven seconds to take leg off including the unfortunate's testicles.

Kid who goes to daughter's school tells me to forget the 67p change. I tell him that every penny counts.

Woman has a turquoise badge of an owl on her lapel. You certainly get more owl badges than Labour Party ones past me.

Cider is purchased. I once knew someone who visited one town in Somerset where the brewery used to put a goat's head into it to prove that it had fermented.

I tell woman that certain Geordie words like 'hoy' meaning *to throw* are derived from Norwegian words.

I discussed with a couple who brought up holiday destinations to avoid. Iraq, I would think, as a holiday destination, could be problematic.   I understand that Columbia is no Frinton and I guess that Burma is not a South East Asian Denmark. I have high hopes for Libya - all that Mediterranean coast line and great Roman remains. I gather Tripoli is an attractive city but things might have changed radically in the last 18 months.

I like the clapping game that young couple were having in the line. Have done it myself with my daughter. Young woman wearing a tee shirt with Roy Lichtenstein image. Liked Warhol and told her about the Tate in Liverpool which is worth a visit.

I like the Canadian woman from Ontario and we chat about Neil Young. She does not mind being thought of as a Yankee unlike someone I know who wears a cap saying that he is Canadian and dislikes being thought of as a Yankee. Curiously he shares this distinction with a woman who came past the till from Arkansas who disliked being thought of as being from north of the Mason-Dixon line.

Woman has Jimmy Choo bag which cost £300. The bloke who bought it is a treasure - a good guy. I like to think that the good guys outnumber the bad guys.

Woman wants me to take care that I note all the reductions on products. Her attitude annoys me - as if I would not. The barcodes have become extremely long and have multiple rows of zeros which make them difficult to read. The husband cackles as I make mistake in entering the numbers. He also leans over which I find annoying. He pays with a £20 note and the bill comes to £11.32. I have no fivers or pound coins as it's about ten minutes from closing and I give him lots of change, or 'slummy' as it's called in Liverpool and he wanders off moaning. I get a frisson of *schadenfreude* at his annoyance.

The local paper was advertising in the jobs section for a court reporter for a post in Truro. That's a hell of a commute.

My first domestic tiff for some time in front of me. The bloke, big, raw-boned farmer type is bullying his rather timid wife (or it could be his sister). I imagine that it will be too much and that one day she will hit him with a shovel and then feed him to the pigs (as long as we don't get the bacon). It will be like a rustic Cluedo with Mrs McGregor killing with a shovel in the cesspit. But only you, dear reader and I will know the truth.

Woman who has done very well from dealing in stamps - it grew out of a hobby. I tell her "Philately will get you everywhere".

Soon after there was a woman enthusing about Jerez and the whole Andalusia thing. With my daughter doing Spanish it's a destination I would like to make and perhaps I will one day.

Spirits rose when chatted at the till with an English student who was a great Joyce fan. She is wading through *Ulysses* at the moment and enjoying it. I told her the anecdote that is in the Richard Ellmann biography of a literary soiree where a devoted Canadian fan approaches Joyce and asks "Can I kiss the hand that wrote *Ulysses*?" To which Joyce rapidly withdrawing hand said "No, it's done other things as well". I chatted about *Portrait of an Artist* which was my first introduction and mentioned the description of the Irish Sea as "snot green and scrotum tightening".

Spoke to woman - a former nurse - who was on a limited income buying many reduced chickens. It's what you have to do to get by when you are on a little money. She also told me that she knew someone with five part-time jobs and I can well believe it.

The Farmer and I had a laugh about the *Daily Express* and its absurd headlines - this one was on the weather. High winds are about to hit the country apparently and next week it will be a heat wave. It's either the climate, Lady Di, ailments or immigrants. The trick will be to combine all elements in one headline. She used to take the *Guardian* and reminisced about some of the great writers of the past like Norman Shrapnel, Terry Coleman and Alistair Cook. It's not so good now as too many North London types write for it. I could not disagree. A *Guardian*-reading farmer, eh? I wonder if there are any *Telegraph*-reading social workers.

We talk about *Strictly Come Dancing* which both my partner and daughter like. I was asked who I thought would win. I plucked a name out of the air and said "Sophie". The couple did not watch *X Factor* and neither do I: "It's like watching the inmates of Bedlam".

I served a delightful Dutch family from Leiden. It goes without saying that I found them perfect in English. Linguistically the Dutch must be the most gifted of nations.

I was chatting about *Annie Get Your Gun*. (The elderly customer was drooling over Betty Hutton). I told him that *Buffalo Bill's Wild West* with Annie Oakley came to the area at least three times from 1891 onwards. My grandfather probably saw it in April 1904.

Dexy's Midnight Runners are giving it some as *Geno* is belting out at the store. Reminded me of the Top Rank and a misspent youth. We talked about the recent documentary on Northern Soul and what a good job Paul Mason did; as a Wiganer he will have an understanding of the music.

Woman who farms in the Dales was telling me of the difficulty that locals have in buying houses even with the 'Local Buy' policy. The last two-bedroom house locally went for over £200,000. Not surprising when social housing was decimated by the 'Right to Buy' policy. People living on low wages in the countryside are in a dilemma.

For some reason Marie Lloyd popped into my head as a customer was telling me about her favourite chocolate - a guilty pleasure. "A little of what you fancy does you good".

Talk to Australian woman about how shopping and especially variety of vegetables have changed since the 70s. I recall the first courgettes and aubergines being sold to bemused customers at that time. The other anecdote I can remember is someone at University telling me that aubergines made his dog - a Boxer - fart.

Spoke to ex-Para. He was in the 6th Army in the War and was in the same places as my father: Caen, Ardennes and the Rhine Crossing. I think Lt General Sir Brian Horrocks was the commanding officer.

At work chatted to a Greek man from Corfu on how perilous the situation was in Greece. It's only 40 years since the Colonels were in power, he reminds me.

We began recalling all those songs that used to be on Family Favourites such as *Nellie the Elephant, Ugly Duckling, Right said Fred, My Brother* with Terry Scott. I felt that we could do with a community sing song of *The King is in the all together.* I feel a moment's silence for Danny Kaye is called for.

Charming ex-country and western singer. Police used to run him in because he travelled back in early hours after a gig and mocked his get up. He adored Don and Hank Williams.

Sautéed onions reminds of comment re Stephen, a dyslexic physicist at York. He later got a job at Aldermaston in radiation research. Joe thought that a misplaced order for Sautéed Onions would cause confusion leading to destruction of Soviet Union.

Middle aged man with cravat and those glasses on a cord - I knew he'd be trouble. He did not talk but just shook his head and grunted. He made a grab for an item and me in my best RSM voice said "Wait for it". It had the desired effect - he recoiled.

Couple buy a copy of *Conan the Barbarian* and shortly afterwards a box of eggs goes past: I open and examine the eggs. "I'm Conan the Ovarian," I say. I am pleased with myself — almost as good as 'philately will get you everywhere' earlier in the week.

Woman eats baby corn before till. "I'm addicted to corn," she says. I may have misheard but then she might just be appallingly honest.

Woman buys a *Top Cat* video. I tell her that it's based on the *Phil Silvers Show* with Top Cat taking the Bilko role. I think Benny the Ball was Duane Doberman. Later a couple buy *Scooby Doo* the original 60s cartoon. They ask me what character I identify with. It is probably Thelma. It's the specs and the sweater that does it for me.

Woman buys many bags of wine gums as partner can only sleep after eating a bag. I'm not interested in psychoanalysis only selling the stuff.

Man wearing 'Jesus is Coming' tee shirt. I doubt whether he will be using local bus service.

Man shopper works in the on-line betting industry. The Chinese market is big: "The Chinese will bet on two spiders climbing a wall".

Man who works for a brick-making company tells me that it employs 26 people when it used to employ 2,000. The bricks are very much in demand for projects in the South of England.

Mentioned Sgt Bilko (after the *Top Cat* encounter) and the episode where Lady Luck has smiled on him and he does not realise it until the last moments of the day. He tries to place a bet on a horse in Australia. I imagine it is easier now with on line betting.

Headline of sensational magazine says
'Undead invade our tents'.
I have seen it myself on a campsite
in North Wales.

Woman works at Aldi tells me that they scan 1000 items a day otherwise questions are asked and they could be got rid of. It seems to me that they are like hamsters on a wheel. Chaplin's *Modern Times* comes into my head.

Elderly man wearing what I correctly guessed was the Arctic Star for working on the convoys to Russia during the war. He was on *HMS Suffolk,* a frigate. I have tremendous respect for people like that as did the bloke behind him who engaged him in conversation long afterwards.

We seem to selling plastic samurai swords. No doubt if sales do not meet the target then staff will commit Seppuku but messily.

Woman going to Silver Wedding celebration, 70th and 18th birthday celebrations as well as engagement all on one day. I feel that such a portmanteau approach to family events would not work with a funeral. It reminded me of the Dave Allen sketch where a Vicar marries an elderly man and a heavily pregnant woman. The man dies and then the woman gives birth.

Last customer and he has taken advantage of lots of rolls for 9p as well as doughnuts and meat pies going for absurdly low prices. I wonder if he is going to have a party. If he is then the mice are not invited as he buys five mouse traps.

Woman has *V.VI.MCMXCII* as tattoo on her neck - it is her date of birth in Roman numerals. However it would not pass as proof of age in Pompeii. "Grates," I say.

Woman works in local court. She tells me of some appalling people that she has to deal with. "But if it wasn't for the riff raff I'd be out of a job". Suggest that *If it wasn't for the Riff Raff* would be excellent title for her autobiography.

Italian woman from Calabria wanted it to be known that she was not from Sicily. She was insistent that I knew that.

Woman told me that she had £500 taken from her account by someone cloning her card whilst buying something on the net.

Man wearing duffle coat. It is some time since I have seen someone in a duffle coat. He bought it on ebay. It was the sort of duffle coat that Jack Hawkins wore in *The Cruel Sea*. The young man lacked a lantern jaw though. I wonder if it was a pipe in the pocket, or was he just pleased to see me?

Several people told me that they had just lost their jobs. One from the DWP said that it was a "bit of a pig" whilst a 53 year old man - a printer - had lost his job with the council and believes he has little chance of getting another one.

Man worried about emigrating to Canada.
He was going to Vancouver, "but have I made the right decision?"
He reassures himself.

Discussed the night class that I run with a customer, as the subject is the Winter of 1947. Winter that year was the worst of the century according to many. One bloke from Grindon said about taking a shovel into the house so they could dig themselves out each morning. Another spoke of the snow above telegraph wires.

Child with his mother, the boy is chatty and he has an Action Man. Reminds me of the Les Dawson joke about extreme poverty in Manchester. So poor that he was given an empty box at Christmas with the words 'Action Man - the deserter'.

One of my favourite blokes, a Scot, came past. We always have a good laugh. We spoke about the British Empire and the hardship of the British standing up to natives armed with vicious guava fruit when they had only highly explosive shells and machine guns. *Blackadder* came into the conversation especially the line about Field Marshal Haig moving his drinks cabinet six inches closer to Berlin as a consequence of the Somme Offensive. We are about to begin the First World War commemoration.

Man tells me he'd seen AC/DC when a light fell off a balcony nearly hitting him. Curiously enough I was told a few days ago of a similar incident that happened at a Yes gig at the same venue in the 70s. There must be a Phantom of the Opera wandering around back stage.

Woman discusses the many ways you can cook with paprika. I have cooked goulash but she uses it in everything. Suggests that she writes cookbook *101 Ways With Paprika*.

Interesting chat with bloke who tells me of his liking for Belgian Jazz. He lived in Ghent for a time working with band. I think he told me that he was the drummer. It was the beer that attracted him. At least he was honest.

Man (he looked like Philip Larkin/John Christie the strangler) very annoyed as we were delayed because woman in front's credit card was playing up. I could feel the heat of the resentment and anger.

Woman tells me about her psychic aunt who can see dead people. More often than not I see stupid ones.

Woman who wears a very large pectoral cross in turquoise. I think it could be Greek Orthodox—it certainly has a Byzantine look about it. Rather splendid, although she is not a regular Church attendee but at least she is sympathetic and she is not as irreligious as the Australian woman who asked for a crucifix with the "little man on".

AISLE THREE

Customer and I deplore the inability of modern youth to read a map. It was mentioned in an *AA* survey where people were unable to distinguish the M5 and the River Severn, with possible alarming and tragic consequences.

A man is trying the three B's diet - beer, bananas and Bell's whisky, that is. He might not lose much weight but he will be happier.

I ask the woman whether she wanted any help, meaning help with her packing: "Setting boundaries and a wayward 21 year old son" was the answer. The Boundaries woman and I then have a good chat about music. She used to date a concert pianist and we discovered a shared liking for John Ogden who I saw at the RFH in '87. She was impressed and she enjoyed the brief conversation.

Discuss the idea of providing poetry as a means of calming people down and did write to Poetry Society without any response. Still think that the idea of a Pindaric Ode from the tills is a good one.

For no obvious reason man tells me at the till that he believes in Reincarnation.

Man on mobile and tilting neck used to insert phone. The wind will change and he will be stuck like that.

Bloke wearing a Wigan Rugby League top. I had forgotten that they no longer play at Central Park. I told him my favourite Wigan joke. A Wiganer wins the Lottery and decides to send son to Eton. After a year goes down to Eton to see how his son Alan is getting on. He sees the Headmaster "How's our Alan doing?" "Reet Champion" replies the Headmaster.

Woman who has named her Baby daughter Francesca. A name of a potential Cambridge graduate she says "unlike Chardonnay," which seems an unnecessarily snobbish thing to say.

Man suggested we have the stocks back. Good idea. We can sell off our over-ripe vegetables as projectiles.

Couple buy Soreen malt loaf. Do they recall the advertising jingle? 'Where's the Soreen, Doreen?' Up there with 'Go to Work on an Egg' and the one that Salman Rushdie did on cream cakes. I suspect Doreen has fallen completely out of favour as a name.

Man tells me that he is off doing the 3 Peak Challenge. On Snowdon last week he saw people tottering around in high heels. I told him that group were training for the first transsexual ascent on Everest.

There are mixed opinions about the new expanded store. One woman vows never to cross the threshold again. People complain that they cannot find their way around the store. Suspect people will moan at anything that involves change. Probably hated the wheel and loathed the steam engine. It's the way around here. "We're not backward, burn the witch".

Early on in the shift and the question of food banks came up and with the first customers there was evident disgust at the remorseless rise of the food bank as a modern day arm of social services. One woman said that it was the fault of people who "spent money on fags". I pointed out that many of the people using them were actually in work and with the price of food going up, plus the costs of energy by about 12%, then it's easy to see how people are running out of money to meet even the basics. I hope I got through.

Chatted to a Policeman about his work and whether it gave him a jaundiced view of human nature. To his credit he said no. He had worked with Scouse colleagues who he deemed worse than the criminals. He also mentioned the programme on Scunthorpe. Is this a fair representation of the poor? I am sure there are people on that estate who are trying to do the decent thing.

Noticed someone - a youth - had 'unapologetic' tattooed on his neck. 'Gormless' would have been more accurate.

Couple were talking about immigrants wanting to take our Christmas over and banning Xmas. I pointed out that the Winterval thing was a commercial concept to extend late year shopping from December right through to February dreamed up, I believe, by the Brummies.

My favourite customer and we spoke about Zappa and he was a great fan of *Hot Rats*. On a walking holiday one of my mates was obsessed with a Zappa track 'Help I'm a rock'. We walked past a loch and my mate would shout out as we passed a boat "Help I'm a boat".

Target culture gets everywhere. I had a job as a Santa once. We had 90 seconds to see each kid, a manager dressed as elf in grotto timed me. She did not make a very good elf.

Wimbledon is upon us. I have little interest in it. When I was at Wigan Health Authority an assistant used to fall mysteriously ill during the period of the tournament. Strange that?

Spoke at work to a woman from Edinburgh who was holidaying in Hull. She must want an Unrest Cure.

I remember Barrie the elderly gay with bouffant hair style who used to get in my local and do Ethel Merman impersonations. He could belt them out. I saw him on a bus the other day. Every hair was in place.

This New Journalism, I tell a customer, is where people write articles for free and it seems all the rage.

I am handed a large bunch of sunflowers to hold for a moment. It could be Provence apart from the lack of sun, the red tiled roofs and the sound of cicadas.

Woman, a retired psychologist, studied at Massachusetts and she knew Sylvia Plath. Visited Plath's grave once; it kept getting vandalised by feminists who objected to Ted Hughes's name being on the stone.

I am reading a comic book on life in a supermarket sent by a friend who lives in Cumbria. Not bad, but not in the same league as the exchange I heard as we finished work the other day. Colleague who has a drag act called *Rhoda the Horse* was complaining about something. He was admonished by another colleague: "Stop being such a drama queen. But you are a drama queen!"

I mention a relative who had been stung when someone in West Africa had helped themselves to their account. The woman I was speaking with said something similar had happened to her father, whose account was accessed by people in Albania.

I wonder why the shape of Mateus bottles? I recall having to draw the shape of the bottle for an art class. Given my daughter's current issues with her school, I reflect on the cynical so-and-so Art teacher at my High School, Richardson, who screwed up my drawing when I was 11 and threw it into a bin to the amusement of the other kids. Fortunately the buffoon did not destroy my interest in Art.

Woman buys the expensive New Zealand honey to put on wound on the tail of her greyhound. I was unaware that Manuka honey had this medicinal effect although she assures me that it does.

Man with Royal Opera badge tries to convince me that opera is not as expensive as it looks, but at £30 for the cheapest ticket it is still too expensive for me.

I witnessed a domestic tiff in front of my till. There is some muttering and hissed comment over alleged unwarranted purchases — in this case washing capsules. I was with the man as the woman seemed to be in advanced faffing mode. I recall a similar annoyance between a couple in Northallerton one New Year's Eve in the 90s at a B&B. The woman I was with thought that they looked like Mrs Slocombe and Captain Peacock.

Ask woman as she buys *Twilight* DVD, "Why are there no ugly vampires?" It's true: you would have thought that at least one would have been plain looking. Although life as a vampire must have its perils. Garlic, stakes, holy water, sunlight, etc. I like the episode in *Dance of the Vampires* with Alfie Bass the Jewish Vampire, on whom the cross had no effect.

Couple are going to Rome for holiday and looking forward to it. The woman is an expert packer and has very good spatial awareness more so than the bloke. I tell them to go to the Capuchin Church with all the bones arranged in patterns. It makes a very effective *memento mori*. I also tell them about the old soldier who ended up in the far north of Italy and enjoyed the end of the war by 'borrowing' an Alfa Romero to visit a knocking shop in Trieste. They still had to face competition from the Americans.

Man told me he used to work at the store until his knee gave way. He says that he is now too old to work. I guess that it is a fate that will befall many.

Woman buys gingerbread for her 30 year old boyfriend who is addicted to the stuff. She thinks he is an imbecile and is very blunt about it.

Man buys a lot of water - 16 flagons of the stuff. It's a long story, but it's about a borehole at a new house in the hills that has not been passed fit for human consumption and there are guests expected over the weekend.

A group of public school boys appear. They are very blond and look distant. They seem like the Midwich cuckoos.
It is all very unsettling.

I mention to a woman the story I intend to write about the young Polish Jewish woman who was found murdered in 1944. The murder was unsolved. The shopper thought it an interesting and worthy project.

Woman buys Horror DVD. She tells me that her husband is a 30 year veteran traumatised by service in the Gulf and Falklands who has a dread of zombies. She thought that she would try to snap him out of his torpor. It seems very radical to me.

Child with wings and he attempts lift off in the store. Would wings be an advantage? No need to use the expensive bus to get to Wakefield and solves parking issues. The Mother and I have a surreal moment and I mention personal helium balloons so you can float over the countryside. Steering and propulsion would be an issue though. You would not like to float over the sea or hit a pylon.

I do like the smell of herbs. The mint on sale was very strong also the rosemary. I am taken back to a Greek monastery I was in on Patmos and the overwhelming smell of rosemary at some religious service. But back to autumn and the chill winds.

Halloween stuff being purchased by the populace and Zombies are a favourite buy. I mention something I saw once about film *Night of the Living Dead* with strap line 'When Hell is full then Zombies will stalk the earth'. In a certain East Yorks city someone had substituted a 'U' for the 'E'.

I overhear one of the young women ask "What's 17 + 4?" A query that is hardly likely to inspire confidence in this counting exercise.

As the rain came down in torrents I asked a woman where she would escape to. She said New Zealand. I took up this theme with others and Australia and New Zealand were most popular. I would like Latin America — the name Valparaiso rather intrigues me, cropping up as it does in so many sea shanties.

I am on stock-taking. It is as tedious as Hell and I
have been given the detergent section. I am
counting bleach, all sort of, and it is
tempting to take a glug.
I wonder what the lemon one tastes like?

It has come to this - the blue toilet blocks. It reminded me of a cartoon that was in a York University Rag Mag circa 1977. It pictured a dazed looking student surrounded by bits of broken toilet. Voice off: "No Rudi - I said smash the system".

I am on air fresheners now and one is called Egyptian Mystique. I am in Anthony Aloysius mode "Are they stark raving mad! Have any of them been to Cairo in July?"

I am handling Shake'n'Vac now. An actor I once knew, Tony Benson, appeared in a Shake'n'Vac advert once in the 80s. But this role is a long way from starring with Richard Burton in the 50s. Tony was also in Corrie as a tram driver and also as a solicitor, although not at the same time. Silly sod did not think you could get AIDS after 50. Tragically, he was proved wrong.

Couple arrive with leg of lamb and I mention the Roald Dahl story about the wife who beats her unfaithful husband to death with frozen leg of lamb and then eats the evidence. Man thinks that this is amusing and might try it on wife. She is unamused, very unamused.

Favourite places is the theme for today's session at the till. Woman loved living in Norway and shed tears when she left. I tell her about my time in Norway in the 70s in Sør-Trøndelag. I say something in the language. I say that I love Wastwater which is the most fjord-like of the Lakes. She agrees.

Woman wears 'Bagpuss' badge. We talk about the work of Oliver Postgate - Noggin the Nog, until he got arrested for it.

A rather sniffy Scottish woman is next, apparently a 'Big Cheese' in the Soroptimist movement. I innocently ask about differences between the Soroptimists and the WI. It was a case of the People's Front for the Liberation of Judaea versus Judanian People's Liberation Front. She got a bit uppity. Now I know.

Did my bit for maintaining the *Entante Cordiale* with three young French men. I said "Bon Soir" as they left.

Man told me that he blindfolds the kids as a game to get them to eat fruit.

Notice that the *Land Rover Magazine* has a front cover with '40 shades of grade' on the front cover. Everyone seem to be getting on the band wagon (or in this case the Land Rover) now.

They are playing *Bring Me Sunshine* over the speaker more in hope than expectation.

I feel that as a checkout operator we could benefit from a bit of collective singing when it gets a bit busy at the tills. I wonder what the punters would think if I burst out with "King Louis was the King of France before the revolution".

Awful haughty *Horse and Hounds* type woman about 35 addresses me as if I am her servant. You can always tell the ones you think will treat you with disdain. I am seething afterwards. Come the revolution I think I know whose house I will expropriate. An *Observer* reader as well. I somehow thought they might know better.

A young man about eight with impeccable manners calls me 'sir' and asks me to stop while his mother gets something. From his manners he looked like Oliver asking for more. I reward him with more tokens. Contrast that with the elderly Irish couple who asked me directions, or rather barked the name of the place they were seeking at me.

My daughter told me that she had heard a news item that 50% of children could not tell the difference between cucumbers and courgettes. We have a problem here where years ago a young trainee had never seen a courgette. I feel we should have a vegetable identification chart in the same way that the Home Guard had German aircraft ID charts in WWII. I see the courgette as the Dornier of vegetables.

Aberdonian. I recall the joke about it being first city in Britain to have double glazing, designed to save money by muffling the sound of passing ice cream vans and ensuring kids did not hear them.

Woman tells me that her old dog has died and the cat that is left spends time looking around the house for his old pal, crying like a baby. The woman says it sets her off every time the cat does it.

Couple buy root beer or sarsaparilla, a stock item in the bars of the Old West. Usually the baddie makes fatal error by assuming that the Alan Ladd character is a sissy for drinking sarsaparilla. The ensuing gun fight proves him wrong. I tell the couple that I will see them back at the ranch and give them extra tokens for allowing to me to relive the tales of the Old West.

The rain gets heavier and a man tells me that he has just returned from swimming. I wondered what stroke he intends to use to swim to the car.

Grandparents and grand daughter work collectively to load and pack their shopping and they work as a team. The young girl, about nine, works hard unloading the trolley. I award her extra tokens for her obvious firm grasp of Marxist Theory of the Division of Labour.

Woman buys carpet and I ask if it's a magic one suggesting that she might want to go the Caribbean. She is a cold and wet climate person and hates heat. She went on a cruise to Norway and thought that the Norwegian crew were too drunk. Finland however would do - all those lakes and forests and damp clime would be most agreeable. I said that I would ring Helsinki Airport so they can expect the carpet.

Couple buy apricots. I ask them in what play do apricots play a significant part? Silence. Tell them it's the *Duchess of Malfi* by Webster. Apricots are buried in dung heap and their consumption is used to ascertain whether Duchess is pregnant. Webster employs some great ways to dispatch his characters. Like the poisoned bible that kills the Cardinal. Wonderful.

A nice elderly gay man who chats with me told me another good story. He used to work for the NHS in London and had met with a number of personalities such as Tony Hancock and Spike Milligan — "a lovely man". I keep telling him to write a book of his life. He told me that he had tea with Kenny Everett which must have been an experience.

Annoying bloke would not respond when I attempted pleasantries at the till. I don't think he realised that I was there. I intend trying Klingon next "nuqneH" or even "Hab SoSlI' Quch!"

Man does big shop with two year old happy and contented. "What's her name?" "Ruby," he says. "Ah, so she's a Ruby Tuesday," I respond.

AISLE FOUR

Another celebrity story was of a man who knew someone who went for a meal at a restaurant and Robbie Williams and his mother were there. He asked people not to take pictures and paid for the meals of all the diners.

I reprised the Levi Jeans advert with that Nick bloke when I changed for work in the laundrette except that I am bald, fat and in my 50s.

One of the regulars is a wonderful woman originally from Isleworth who told me once about Hammersmith Palais, where she met her husband. I saw her today and mentioned Hammersmith Palais. She said "You're the only perisher who knows where I'm from". I've never been called a perisher before.

Shoppers who like pork pies. So do I, but buying a dozen of them seems to me to be a bad case of chasing the jelly. I ask them whether they holiday in Melton Mowbray.

I have engaging chat with woman about Radio 2. She likes Jonathan Ross as well as the Irish replacement. She does not like Paul O'Grady who I think is very good. Strange tastes some people. I tell her seven year old son that one of the trolley lockers is a portal to Narnia.

Discuss names with woman with baby called Joseph. I wonder where names like Jaden and Madison came from. I mention that a friend of mine who teaches has a student Helen Highwater. "Courtney, where did that name spring from?" I say "Cash back?" we are at that part of the transaction. She thinks I'm on my names rant. "Cash...back, I have never heard of that name". Explain I'm offering cash back. Lor how we roared.

The guy who always talks about 70s bands was in the other day and talking about Pink Fairies, a band I have never heard of. He mentioned the album *Uncle Harry's Last Free Coat*. "Not many people have heard of them now, mind you few had heard of them at the time," he remarked.

A man questions me on the effectiveness of an electric iron he has just purchased. I tell him to follow the instructions, especially the one about not wearing a shirt when ironing it as this can cause burns.

Couple tell me the cost of their daughter's Prom. It will cost £1,000, including £300 for a dress. Are they serious? Yes, they are. Father thought way out of the cost was to get girl expelled the year before.

I hold on to a bottle of gin for too long and the woman shopper wonders if I want the gin for myself. I say I am a reincarnated Kansas temperance movement circa 1890 and I recall the Mencken quote about Puritanism "the haunting fear that somebody, somewhere is enjoying themselves". Like the man who told me that he hid his empties because of the possibility of neighbour disapproval. Strong Methodists you see.

A woman customer and I were sharing a love of Greece. She liked Crete and I was talking about Patmos and the smell of rosemary in the cave where the *Book of Revelation* was written.

I am convinced that the path to happiness lies in being engaged in some creative process. I was at another job, which is working with people with mental health problems getting them work ready. We had an artist and we were writing poetry. I wrote one of seeing a canvas of some Alpine scenery. I was telling someone at the tills that engaging in something is the route to salvation.

I overheard a young man in the café say that
"She shot me four times in the head".
I think they were talking about paint ball game.

Had conversation with football supporter about past heroes. I said that I had gone into Sportswrite in Manchester about 1998 and asked for a new biography of Len Shackleton. Shackleton was regarded by my father as the greatest player he ever saw at Maine Road. The bloke in the shop did not have a clue who he was. I wonder in 50 years time whether people will look blank when Beckham's name is mentioned.

Beer called Alhambra. I think it's excellent that a beer is named after a mosque.

Woman has a leather coat which she bought locally, which had a design that suggested that it was made of leaves - it looked very effective.

Woman with paint-splattered hair decorating Mum's house. She tells me of the colour scheme she is using - it suggests to me a Peruvian brothel.

Stacking shelves of Christmas goodies. I was on biscuits and followed the diagram which included tins of Scottish Shortbread on the top shelf which were unsteady and liable to brain some unsuspecting shopper with a tin bearing a picture of Eilean Donan Castle. I know death hath ten thousand several doors For men to take their exits; and `tis found, They go on such strange geometrical hinges.

It is slow on till 3 and the ever-engaging Terry on till 1 and I swap banter about how we can get customers to our tills as we are at the far end of the store. I suggest to Tom that we adopt the manner of fairground barkers. "Roll on up and see the bearded lady". A customer unkindly suggests that she is on till 8. And as for the Boneless Wonder...

Woman buying the *Telegraph* used to read the *Guardian*, but thinks *Telegraph* is better paper. She is of liberal views and presumably reads the *Telegraph* in the way that Evelyn Waugh read the *New Statesman* to build up a head of outrage. Mind you if you wanted to feel anger then you would read the *Daily Mail*. It ought to have 'We supported Fascists' on its masthead.

Woman wants me to check her empty bags. I have never done this and will not. She says she had to do this when she shopped in the States. She lived in Glastonbury, Connecticut for several years and this is what they did. Do they think all shoppers are thieves?

I suggest to a man who was struggling with inserting the card into the machine that it was a form of intelligence test and that he had failed.

Man with sweatshirt with the words 'Ah mon genoux' explains that he damaged his knee whilst climbing two years ago in the French Alps. It was near a serac and he explains what exactly one is - an ice overhang. Strangely this is the second time I have heard this word. I heard this morning on Radio 4 discussion on a terrible accident on K2 when several climbers were killed when a serac gave way.

Man buys strong beer made by JW Lees of Manchester. It's 7.8% proof: very much a case of Goodnight Vienna if you drink too much of this or at the very least Goodnight Crumpsall.

Grumpy man wearing a 'Led Zeppelin' tee shirt who I saw in the early 70s. He does not engage with me which is a pity as I had a few anecdotes.

The next one over the speaker *Strut Your Funky Stuff*. I doubt it. And the next one up is *Tiger Feet* and all of a sudden it's 1974.

It seems Bin Laden has been stopped by cops for speeding in Pakistan. I suspect those videos he watched as shot by Navy Seals were old *Top Gear* progs.

Woman said that she could not get her lemon tree to produce fruit. I suggested she play music to them as suggested by the Prince of Wales. I gather Bach works well on trees.

The music playing over the supermarket speaker is *Hotel California* "you can check out any time you like but you can never leave" - scary.

A customer recounted her experience on LSD. A tune-in, drop-out although in this case she thought she had turned into a vampire. I used to work with someone who used to drop a tab of acid whilst in the Chiselhurst Caves - a favourite mod hangout in the 60s. He spent hours looking at an orange.

Told a friend at work the following anecdote which I read in the Michael Sandel book on *Justice* on the folly of utilitarianism and cost benefit analysis. In the 70s, there were complaints that men were staying overnight at St Anne's College, Oxford. The traditionalists were appalled and decided to apply a charge after carrying out a cost/benefit analysis of the impact of having males staying at the College. They decided to charge men 50p per night with a maximum of three nights' stay. The *Guardian* heard about this and ran the headline "ST ANNE'S GIRLS 50p A NIGHT!"

Man likes history and tells me that we are in thrall to a world conspiracy. Brace myself in case he mentions either Jews or Lizards.

Spoke to a teacher from a local school. She taught English and had never heard of Wordsworth!

Irish guy buys condoms. Are they available in the Republic? Reminded me of anecdote when issue of contraception was debated in the Dail in the 30s, against the wishes of the Catholic hierarchy. Bright Senator proposed a ruse to get past ban which was accurate, vague and patriotic as well - suggested they call condoms Roger Casements. A good story if true.

Sold a Goblin suet meat pudding which now comes in plastic not in the tin that you used to punch at the top otherwise the thing tended to explode as it was boiled. I wonder what the casualty rate was from the exploding ordnance as metal, suet and hot gravy flew around the kitchen? There might be a monument at the National Memorial Arboretum for the fallen victims of the Goblin. Just a thought.

Talk about alcohol and the prohibition with knowledgeable bloke. Feel however we might find it difficult to shift drink called *Panther Piss*.

People buy £400 of shopping. I ask if they are feeding the Brigade of Guards, mention to the next shopper a woman who bursts out laughing. Her toddler burst out laughing as well. Result.

Young woman is wearing fine ethnic necklace which she has bought locally. Suggest to her that she try a bit of imagination and tell the next person who asks that she bought it in a Moroccan souk or a stall in Lhasa.

Couple buy greengages. I don't think I have ever tasted them myself. Woman tells me that they are not in season long and they taste like plums. Anyway it's a first for me today. There was a book called *The Greengage Summer* made into a film with Kenneth More. If memory serves me right a sort of Home Counties *Lolita*.

Woman tells me that she is off to a Buddhist retreat for the weekend. I notice that she had a bottle of whisky with her. Surely that cannot be an aid to meditation?

Did laugh at the reminiscence of Bernard Cribbins appearing with Peter Cushing in *Dalek Invasion Earth 2150* with Cushing as Dr Who - I saw it sometime in the early 60s—both men 'corpsing' as the lead Dalek had an Aussie accent. I recount this to someone who buys Dr Who annual.

I informed a customer that the first coffee house was opened in Oxford in the 1650's by a couple of Jews. Cromwell allowed the Jews back after they had been booted out by Edward I in the 1290's because he wanted to renege on loans they had raised for him I presume for funding the building of all those castles in North Wales.

Man who used to work at GEC Stafford recalls visit of Malenkov ex-Soviet premier in 1954 and the heavies with him. He had a problem with security people after that.

I was in conversation with a reader of the *Telegraph* and the subject of obituaries was raised which I think the *Telegraph* does very well. I certainly recall the one about Barbara Cartland which I thought very funny. The libidinous Major who invited the innocent Barbara into his bedroom to show her how his revolver worked. The pink elaborate construction of tulle and taffeta and the plastered make-up and the proud boast that in 1981 being anointed Achiever of the Year by the National Home Furnishing Association of Colorado Springs.

Another Scot, supports Aberdeen but from Portree. Told him the double glazing/ice cream van joke. I wonder if they still practise the cure for depression on Skye where well-meaning friends take the unwell person on a boat trip on a loch and at a given signal throw them into loch. The shock cheers them up... it is said. I wonder whether the local park lake could be pressed into service.

A bell-ringer at the local RC Church engages me in conversation. His first act was to play *Angelus* on bells for previous bell-ringer. Thought this was a rather Thomas Hardy moment.

Quoted H Belloc to man at till who cut his hand after trying to remove an exhaust with a saw. "Lord Acton tried to mend a light, It struck him dead - It serves him right. It is the duty of the wealthy man, To give employment to the artisan."

Recall Brian, who was something of a know-all - God bless him. He fitted his own central heating and died from CO poisoning when he switched it on one night about 30 years ago.

A woman tells me that her company is losing workers: there were 60 last year and now down to seven. They work in construction and the market is not reviving.

Next customer, a postal worker, tells me that every day they try to undermine the terms and conditions of the workers. The pendulum of the power of trade unions stands opposite of where it was in the 70s and the view of us both that it's swung far too much the other way.

A woman (she was in her late 40s) told me and the old man behind her about her father in the Parachute Regiment who took part in a battle in the Ardennes, which took place in January 1945. Incidentally that was where my father was. In fact, he was bombed by a ME 262. The woman was trying to put the history of her father's war together. He had died in 2002. The old man and the woman embraced. I felt that it was a rather touching incident.

Young woman has a tee shirt with picture of Lugosi as Dracula. I did the impersonation "I do not drink wine" and her male companion looked blankly at me. I sense no humour there.

The old man told me that he was approaching 90. I asked him about the war. He was in a Northern Ireland Regiment - the Royal Enniskillen Dragoon Guards and the Earl of Kildare was his commanding officer. He was in D-Day and was near the Pegasus Bridge. He told me how bitter he was in the way the country had turned out.

African - A Ghanaian perhaps? Pill box hat, baggy shirt, and black pallium carrying silver top cane in store. Not usual local sight and he gets smirks and nods from the locals. A colleague talks about goats being tethered outside. I inwardly wince.

Woman buys lots of bottles of vinegar and tells me that she is making up fly spray with vinegar, old tea and oil of citronella. She has several Shetland ponies which she believes are a much misunderstood equine. They are the strongest horse for their respective size. I tell her the story of Joe Derbyshire, a friend from Wigan. I visited him in hospital shortly before he died. He told me that as a young boy he worked with the pit ponies. During the 1921 strike, ponies were brought to the surface and lived in fields beside the pit. When the strike ended, they were rounded up to go down the pit. Joe remembered the ponies whinnying in terror at the prospect of returning underground. It's a tale that has always lived with me.

Woman has an exotic necklace with cartouche of Isis. I have a fear that a Mummy will lumber into the store shortly looking for reincarnation.

I think people make assumptions about supermarket staff. Some months ago, a bloke made a comment about my education having "got you where you are". I did think of saying my Fellowship of All Souls was, on reflection, a bad thing. I work with many interesting people, including a bloke who used to be in the Merchant Navy and was a radio officer on ships going to Vietnam during the war.

At till, I come up with 'False badge Syndrome' - people wandering around with ID. Suggest shoppers wear bogus ones such as FBI, NASA or Illuminati just to confuse people.

A customer tells me that Wilmington, Delaware is no great shakes. I cannot comment but it starts an 'ear worm' as I hum the Dean Martin song about a "brand new jersey".

Express has headline 'A Cure for dementia'.
The solution is simple -
stop reading the *Express*.

I chat to a charming couple. He was a miner from Swadlincote and 16 at the time of D-Day. He recalled seeing the fires engulfing Coventry about 40 miles away.

Man wearing 'Okinawa' tee shirt got from Primark with unknown Japanese ideogram which possibly translates as 'Fat Western bastard'.

"I'm 92," the woman says. She tells me about her war work on munitions and making incendiary bullets for the RAF, where she met her husband.

Bloke has *Times*. "How long have you been reading the paper?" I ask. He told me that his daughter's school thought that she should be reading a more edifying paper that would be good for her education. That was about 30 years ago. He used some money from a business sell-off to play the Stock Exchange and took the *Times* for advice, concentrating on Far East markets and consequently making £2million. Not bad, eh?

The conversation concerns a newly opened Waitrose in a nearby town. A woman tells me that her friend uses the one in Romsey in Hampshire and is rather snobbish about it. Lidl she dismisses as the place where poor people go.

A Sikh man dressed in a penguin tee shirt—Fathers' Day present, he says. I tell him that 'penguin' is a Welsh word meaning 'white head'. He grins and pats his white turban.

Man tells me there's "nothing worse than queuing". Well, there is actually, I say. There now follows a list: Black Death, terminal illness, nuclear warfare, indeed all warfare, redundancy, earthquakes, major flooding incidents, famine, etc.

A Woman who is wearing 'Patti Smith' tee shirt. In 1977 she was trying to be a punk but her Mam would not let her.

At my till today were a couple of blokes who worked at the local outdoor centre. My mate Greg used to work there many years ago taking youths from the area rock climbing, while the teacher ('Piggy') used to sit in the van all day reading his copy of the *Mirror,* with three meat pies and a flask of tea.

An elderly man buys a lot of ice cubes. I ask whether he has murdered someone and was preserving the body. He says it might lead to that as he is having a party - a birthday party. He asks me to guess his age. I say 70. He is actually 90 and could easily pass for 20 years younger. Turns out he flew Wildcats in the Fleet Air Arm in Second War in the Med and Norway. Much respect.

A man comes past me and he has chicken. He is having chicken and a curry sauce. He tells me that his wife is a vegetarian and is away at a conference which allows him to smuggle meat into the house. It is a secret pleasure. Poor sod! He probably has to bury the bones in the garden afterwards. It's the tyranny of the lentil, I think. I tell a woman who says "He must be henpecked". "Well, it is chicken", I reply.

Man with moustache with waxed ends. Wonder if the Kaiser look is becoming fashionable. They will be invading Belgium next.

Young woman who is wearing unusual combination of keffiyeh and bowler hat. It's a case of the PLO meeting the Orange Order.

Speculate angry woman who was furious about something was angry because she had a scrape in car, lost her job or discovered her husband had run off with a Swedish sea captain called Sven.

Man from Brazil says he misses the local delicacy that involves doing something with catfish.

Another conversation yesterday at work was the correct way to pronounce the county town of Shropshire. Is it SHREWS bury or is it SHROWS bury? My mate Neil who is from Shrewsbury thinks that it's a class argument - the middle class incomers going for the latter way - and the right way is Shrewsbury. "After all," he told me, with impeccable logic "the play is not the *Taming of the Shrow*". I did see a match once at the unlikely named Gay Meadow where Stoke got soundly beaten by the Shrews. They used to employ someone in a coracle to fish the ball out of the River Severn which runs by the old ground.

Yesterday at the till I was chatting to a customer about the drinking habits of airline pilots. He claimed to know someone who worked as a nanny for a pilot who liked a drink - in fact he needed a bevy to assist him in the cockpit.

Woman tells me that she handed in a wallet she found in street. Proof, I think, of the fundamental honesty of most people in the area.

The John Lennon song *Whatever gets you through the night* I gave as an 'ear worm' to a guy originally from Vancouver as he ambles past tonight. The bastard retaliated with *Yummy, yummy yummy, I've got love in my tummy.* Unforgivable.

Man tells me that he used to play double bass at private parties. I was hoping for something louche but, no. I was rather disappointed.

"Whatever happened to the customer is always right?" I say that cliché died in 1973 about the same time as the oil crisis and Gary Glitter.

I mention that I have in the past scored highly on insubordination. Not the sort of point to suggest as a weakness at job interview.

Woman buys bottle of vodka for school. "Before or after the Ofsted inspection?" I ask.

In a conversation about eels, woman thinks that a young eel is an Elvis. Phrase, 'Elvis has left the river' has a certain ring I think.

Man runs Zombie Adventure Park where out of work actors chase punters. It's in Macclesfield. What does that tell us?

Man commutes long distances and we discuss radio stations. Radio 6 gets positive report but Radio 1 does not. Very much a case of hang the DJ as far as that station is concerned.

Conveyer belt mysteriously breaks down and woman customer trills "Things always stop when I stand beside them". I point at her "Burn the witch".

Woman wearing a 'badger' tee shirt. I asked about Krebs Report and said it was not a black or white issue.

I thought that the woman was French and said a few words. She wasn't, although she was fluent. She asked me what country she was from and gave me five guesses. Czech? No. Hungarian. I was getting closer. Rumanian? Next country to Rumania, she said Bulgaria was incorrect and only one guess. Moldova? Correct. I felt pleased.

Film Noir came into the conversation as the man was thinking of taking insurance out on his wife. Thinking of *Double Indemnity*.

The woman wants to make faffing into a national movement. I suggest a *Born to Faff* tee shirt and re-writing the political philosophy of the greats to accommodate this aspiration. *Man is born free but faffs all the time* or *Faffers of the world unite* or even *Faff Off*.

Man originally from Leeds tells me about the City in the 70s and what a hard place it was. I did see Dennis Healey on the platform of Leeds Station when he was Chancellor in 1978. I seem to remember thinking at the time that he had no security.

I am told off by grumpy looking woman who complains that I am going too fast. "It's not Aldi," she grumbles. I notice she is wearing a tee shirt that says 'Made in Norton'. Why would you boast about this? My mate Greg, years ago, was standing at a bus stop in Norton on which there was a poster from the Tunisian Tourist Board which proclaimed 'In your dreams you are in Tunisia'. Someone had written underneath 'And in your nightmares you are in Norton - land of hope and mither'.

Shrubs appear on belt - two of them. "Birnam Wood to high Dunsinane Hill shall come". Bloke says did not expect such intelligence from supermarket workers. Put him straight.

On the subject of Teddy bears, the woman in her 80s wants to be buried with the one she has had since childhood.

A French woman from Toulouse, a Spanish woman from Castille and a German woman from Weimar - all language tutors in the town. I have visited Weimar and spoke of Bach and Goethe. All she wanted to talk about was the fact that Ravensbruck Concentration Camp was near Weimar. I did not mention the war but she was the one. It reminded me of Jurgen, the Harry Enfield character who wants to apologise all the time.

I was talking to a customer about my father who was a railway porter after the war. He was tipped once by the opera singer Gigli who was a mate of Mussolini and also sang for Hitler. So if my father met Gigli that means I am three degrees of separation from Hitler if you apply the 'degrees of separation from Kevin Bacon' test.

Huskisson Street in Liverpool came into the conversation. I recall in January '79 looking down on a Bruegelesque snowy scene on the Embassy Club from 101 Huskisson Street when the local police launched a raid on the club/brothel as punters attempted an escape in a blizzard with trousers around ankles.

I told man that I did a talk on poverty. Man said that I should leave my pay slips to my descendents so that they can know it existed now.

Woman told me that she was caught up into the Ladbrooke Grove Crash of 8th October 2000. I suppose the date would be etched into my memory as well. She was asleep and the coach was suddenly filled with smoke and flame. She was OK apart from broken specs. She nursed a woman who had blood coming from her mouth and they were both blackened by the smoke.

My much missed mate Jim recalled as a lad in 1967 meeting an old geezer in a Cotswold Church who had asked if he knew what happened to his ancestor, Sir Edmund Verney, at the Battle of Edgehill in 1642. The answer was he was killed and his hand had to be hacked off the Royal Standard. The old man was Sir Harry Verney, the last survivor of the Asquith Government which took us to war in 1914.

Young man attempted to convert me today.
He gave me a homily about JC and a
£1 million Eternity note with
'THIS IS NOT LEGAL TENDER' on it.

Woman believes in angels and that she has one. Mine probably needs dismissal on the grounds of incompetence.

A Black woman wearing a Red Flamingo headgear and collecting for a wildlife charity. She is very happy about a tedious task which she sets to with enthusiasm. A customer tells me that Flamingos are pink and the colouring is down to them eating shrimps. I don't think they are naturally red unless they have been eating beetroot or embarrassed.

Two people buy card for someone 100. It is the second time in a week and another sign of the growth of extreme old age in our society.

The subject of devilled kidneys came up and the woman told me that her father had the dish while on a rough crossing around the Outer Hebrides with the only other person breakfasting being the Captain. He told his wife about the kidneys and she was ill again.

Chatted to elderly chap from Oldham. He thought that we were born in the wrong time. He would like to be have been born in his home town at the start of the 20th century. I suggested 1902, too young for WWI and too old for WWII. Come to think of it a famous son of Oldham was born in 1902 - Sir William Walton. As it happened, the man was taught music by his brother 'Polly' Walton at Oldham Grammar School. He told me that he was a nasty piece of work.

Bloke. He says he knows the dates of all the Monarchs of Britain "Try me" he says, "give me a date". I say 1618. He says Jacobus. He is correct - James I . He collects coins. He's also a *Dad's Army* nut. I give him another date 1388. "Ricardus". Again, he is correct - Richard II. I am trying him on the Popes next time.

Horrible kid playing around with the belt and with the card holder. He told me "Faster, faster" and was generally misbehaving. I felt like saying to the Mother "How long has Damien been possessed?" Reminded me of a mate who thought of a service for ineffectual parents – *Dial-a-Bollocking* – 'We bollock up hill and down dale' was its strap line. It was based on a social worker he knew who had a certain way with truculent kids in care.

Tourist from Louth in Lincolnshire and she works for the company as a checkout operator. It gave me the opportunity to compare notes. She did not like women teachers as customers. Invariably they think they are superior. She liked elderly couples from outlying villages and the fact that you could build a rapport with them. Rather followed my thinking. She did say that they had an irate customer who hurled a Swede - vegetable rather than nationality - down the aisle. Perhaps it's a Lincolnshire custom?

Man waxes long on the beauty of fennel and its versatility. I have never tried it although I gather it tastes of aniseed. I could be a willing convert as he told me how he was introduced to fennel by someone who put it in a salad but, once tasted, he was trying every way to eat the thing - baked, boiled, roasted and today he was having it in a risotto. He told me that the Anglo Saxons were keen on it. Anyway definitely a missionary for Foeniculum.

I open plastic bags for oldish, slightly raffish looking man. He is appreciative and thanks me. For some reason John Lennon comes into the conversation. It turns out that this man was in the same hotel in Montreal that John and Yoko had their sleep-in way back in 1969. For a minute I thought that he was going to tell me that he was in the Plastic Ono Band. I thought from bagism to plastic bagism in one easy movement.

Life of Pi is out on DVD. I tell woman with straight face that it was filmed on location in Wigan. She believes me. The next woman in line realises my joke and says that "There is nothing exotic about Wigan". How little she knows - I think parts of Standish are very bohemian.

I suspect that someone in head office who puts together the music that is played in the store has a wry sense of humour. Over my cuppa in the Canteen I heard the sound of *People are Strange* by the Doors. I am not sure whether it is meant for the staff or the customers. If the latter can I suggest *People are Strange (Especially Hill Farmers)* to be played on Tuesdays when its market day.

UNEXPECTED ITEM IN THE BAGGING AREA

The bill came to £19.75. On the subject of 1975, in my researches I came across the diverting story of Irishman Mr Dooley of Stoke who had an unfortunate incident when a squirrel ran up his trouser leg and exited at his shirt. The animal bit him on the left ear lobe. Fortunately the squirrel was not interested in Dooley's goolies.

Parent put small child on conveyor belt by my till. The toddler was highly delighted but I politely told the parent that the child might get its fingers trapped in the belt. He lifted the bairn off. I have a sense as far as possible hazards are concerned; it comes with being the oldest of five. The stupidest thing I ever saw was at a commune in Dorset in 1988. I was helping out in the kitchen and there was an infant standing on a chair by a stove on which was a boiling pan of water. I moved the child away but the prat of a Dad rebuked me for moving them, saying that if the child was scalded then it would be a "learning experience". It's not only the feckless on benefits that should be marked out for crap parenting. The Middle Class are equally likely to screw up.

Man wandered by my till. Concerned not to be taken for a shoplifter, he offered to show me the contents of his bag. "Would you like to see my brother's plums?" I declined his kind offer.

Overheard woman at work talk about someone being obese and having an attitude problem. I was unsure whether she was talking about a dog or her husband. Then she mentions castration and the mystery is solved.

"That's shallot" I say, as the last item is scanned. They missed my comment, but raved about the humble vegetable.

I will leave the very last word to my wonderful 10 year old daughter who, during a recent trip out, volunteered her policies if she were ever to become Prime Minister: she would pass a law that people had to be polite to each other, increase wages and have more BOGOF offers, Watch this space...

ABOUT THE AUTHOR

Bill Cawley is a man of eclectic taste and knowledge. His sojourns into the realm of the paranormal somehow manage to juxtapose eloquently with an entanglement of historical narrative and wry observational commentary on twenty-first century behaviour across all sections of society.

Why would a degree-wielding, Mastermind contestant, community activist, former Councillor and ex-Santa want to record his pithy mental meanderings for posterity? His current post as leader of the 'smile at them all, regardless' checkout operatives gives him the opportunity to simply sit back and take the money.

Not Bill Cawley, though! No, he uses his time wisely and with an eye to the future wealth creation of his keenly honed mind's output.

He is also completely nuts, and under any other government which funded the NHS properly, would have been sectioned by now - but let's not dwell on the negative. He is currently working on his next book, *Shadows of the Past*, an anthology of his writings on the Staffordshire moorlands.

ALSO BY TMB BOOKS

FORGOTTEN LANCASHIRE AND PARTS OF CHESHIRE AND THE WIRRAL

"Comic genius or woeful local history"
Lancashire Life

"The antidote to local history books"
Linghams Books

"A dozen laughs a page"
Wigan Observer

"A wonderful, majestic tour de force"
Nataya Ripley

THE LOST FILMS OF 20th CENTURY SPATCHCOCK

"Worth saving up £9.99 for"
Martin Sixsmith

"At last—the definitive appreciation of Spatchcock! Anyone who has managed to get through From Here To Maternity or Wendy Does Wigan will want - and need - this book."
Andy Kershaw

"Hilarious!"
Billy Butler, BBC Radio Merseyside

Available from all good bookshops or from online book stores.

Made in the USA
Charleston, SC
08 October 2014